ISLE OF SCILLY

TRAVEL GUIDE

2023 - 2024

A definitive guide to explore one of the UK's hidden jewels, the lovely Isles of Scilly.

Kenneth Finley

Copyright

TABLE OF CONTENTS

About This Guide

Welcome to the Isles of Scilly Travel Guide for 2023-2024! This thorough book is your passport to explore one of the UK's hidden jewels, the lovely Isles of Scilly. Whether you're a first-time tourist or returning for another adventure, this guide is meant to improve your experience and make your travel unique.

Benefits of This Guide:

- **Up-to-date Information:** Our guide is painstakingly researched and continuously updated to give you the most recent information. From travel limitations to newly found sights, we've got you covered.

- **Customized Itineraries**: We provide professionally created itineraries that suit a range of interests and trip lengths. Whether you're seeking leisure, outdoor excursions, or cultural encounters, our itineraries help you make the most of your time on the islands.

- **Insider Tips**: Benefit from local insights and ideas that go beyond the conventional tourist destinations. Discover secret beaches, dine at small cafes, and discover off-the-beaten-path wonders.

- **Practical guidance**: Navigate your travel with ease owing to practical guidance on transportation, lodging, and necessary services. We advise on anything from packing basics to currency exchange.

- **Event revisions:** Stay updated about exceptional events, festivals, and unique experiences occurring on the Isles of Scilly in 2023 and any revisions for 2024. Don't miss out on the rich local culture.

- **Safety and Health Tips**: Your well-being is our focus. Find vital safety information, emergency contacts, and health suggestions to ensure worry-free travel.

- **Sustainability Focus:** Discover eco-friendly practices and responsible tourism tips to help you enjoy and maintain the natural beauty of the Isles of Scilly.

- **Inspiration**: Get inspired by breathtaking photographs, tales, and traveler experiences to fire your wanderlust and make the most of your visit to this great place.

With this book in hand, you're ready to start on a remarkable vacation to the Isles of Scilly, where rocky beaches, crystal-clear seas, and friendly hospitality await. Embrace the charm of these secluded islands and create lifetime memories. Your journey starts here!

I. INTRODUCTION

A. About the Isles of Scilly

Nestled in the blue seas of the Celtic Sea, the Isles of Scilly are a group of picturesque islands off the southwestern coast of England. This archipelago, including over 140 islands, is a hidden treasure recognised for its pure natural beauty, gorgeous beaches, and a distinct feeling of tranquility. Often referred to as the "Sunny Isles" owing to their mild temperature, the Isles of Scilly provide a mesmerizing retreat from the rush and bustle of contemporary life.

B. Travel Guide Purpose

The objective of this trip guide is to act as your ultimate companion while experiencing the Isles of Scilly in 2023-2024. Whether you're a a solitary traveler, a couple seeking a romantic retreat, a family in search of adventure, or just a nature lover, this book is meant to appeal to your requirements and interests.

Our objective is to give you extended, up-to-date, and accurate information to make your vacation to the Isles of Scilly memorable. From organizing your vacation and traversing the islands to immersing yourself in local culture and natural beauty, this book is your entrance to an outstanding experience.

C. Tips for Travelers

As you begin on your trip to the Isles of Scilly, here are some helpful advice to guarantee a smooth and pleasant adventure:

- **Timing Is Everything**: Consider going in late spring or early summer when the weather is pleasant, and the flora and wildlife are in full bloom. This is the best time for outdoor exploration and beachcombing.

- **Travel Light**: The Isles of Scilly have a casual environment, so bring comfortable clothes, sunscreen, a rain jacket, and strong walking shoes for exploring the rocky landscape.

- **Book Accommodations Early:** Accommodations might fill up fast, particularly during peak season. Booking in advance guarantees you have your pick of hotels, B&Bs, or self-catering cottages.

- **Respect Nature**: The natural beauty of the Isles is its greatest asset. Be responsible in traveling to conservation initiatives, abstaining from harming animals, and following the "Leave No Trace" ideals.

- **Visit Beyond St. Mary's:** While St. Mary's is the main island and provides numerous activities, don't miss the chance to visit the smaller, calmer islands like Tresco, St. Martin's, and Bryher, each with its distinct charm.

- **Try Local Cuisine**: Savor the tastes of the Isles by indulging in fresh seafood, Scillonian produce, and locally created delights. Visit local eateries and bars to immerse yourself in the island's gastronomic culture.

- **Plan for Activities**: If you have certain activities in mind, such as diving, kayaking, or guided tours, it's preferable to schedule them in advance to reserve your position.

- **Embrace Island Time**: The Isles of Scilly function at a slower, more leisurely pace. Embrace this island time and allow yourself to relax, disengage, and absorb in the tranquil ambience.

With these recommendations in mind, you're well-prepared to go on your adventure to the Isles of Scilly. This travel book will follow you every step of the journey, helping you explore the hidden gems and experiences that make this location so special. Get ready to immerse yourself in the charm of the Isles of Scilly.

II. PLANNING YOUR TRIP

A. When to Visit

Choosing the correct time to visit the Isles of Scilly is key for a great trip. In 2023-2024, the archipelago provides diverse charms throughout the year.

- **Spring (March to May)**: This season is good for nature enthusiasts and hikers. Witness the islands' wildflowers in full bloom, including bright bluebells and pink thrift. The weather is warmer, making it great for outdoor exploring.

- **Summer (June to August):** The Isles of Scilly come alive in summer. Days are longer, and the sun shines brilliantly, making it excellent for beach days and water sports like kayaking and snorkeling. Note that this is the high tourist season, so lodgings and activities may fill up fast.

- **Fall (September to November)**: Early fall is a terrific time to visit while the weather is still decent, and the summer crowds have begun to subside. It's a fantastic season for birding and enjoying the islands' serenity.

- **Winter (December to February):** While the winter months are quieter, they provide a distinct and calm experience. Stroll along deserted beaches, cuddle up in island bars, and enjoy the tranquil beauty of the Isles. Keep in mind that certain shops may shut for the season, so plan appropriately.

B. How to Get There

Getting to the Isles of Scilly includes a combination of transportation modes:

- **By Air:** The most frequent method to access the Isles is by taking a short flight from Exeter, Newquay, or Land's End Airport to St. Mary's Airport. Flights are available year-round, with additional alternatives during the peak season.

- **By Sea:** You may also access the Isles by boarding a passenger ferry from Penzance to St. Mary's. This leisurely drive provides stunning coastline vistas but takes longer than a flight.

C. Visa and Entry Requirements

Traveling to the Isles of Scilly, being part of the UK, typically follows the same admission criteria. If you're a British citizen or a citizen of a European Union (EU) or European Economic Area (EEA) nation, you may visit the Isles with a valid passport or identification card. However, it's crucial to check for any updates or changes to immigration and visa laws before your travel, since they might alter.

For tourists from non-EU/EEA countries, visa restrictions may apply. Ensure that you investigate and secure the relevant visas or permissions well in advance of your trip date.

D. Packing List

Packing carefully ensures you're prepared for the various weather and activities on the Isles of Scilly. Here's a list of essentials to consider:

- **eWeather-appropriate gear:** Dress in layers, including waterproof gear for anticipated rain showers. Comfortable, moisture-wicking apparel for outdoor activities is essential.

- **Footwear**: Sturdy walking shoes or hiking boots for visiting the islands, as well as flip-flops or sandals for beach days.

- **Sun Protection:** Sunscreen, sunglasses, and a wide-brimmed hat to shelter oneself from the sun's rays.

- **Swimwear**: If you wish to swim or enjoy water sports, bring your swimwear and a beach towel.

- **Electronics**: Chargers, adapters, and a power bank for your electronics, as well as a camera to record the breathtaking scenery.

- **Travel Documents:** Passport, identity, airplane or ferry tickets, and any applicable visas.

- **Personal prescriptions:** Any prescription prescriptions you need, along with a basic first-aid kit.

- **Cash and Cards**: A combination of cash and credit/debit cards for expenditures, since certain locations on the islands may not take cards.

E. Travel Insurance

Before leaving on your journey, it's vital to invest in comprehensive travel insurance. This insurance should cover travel cancellations, medical crises, lost bags, and other unexpected circumstances. Given the Isles' remote position, getting good travel insurance guarantees you're financially protected and can obtain the required help in case of problems.

Remember to check the insurance carefully to understand the coverage and any limitations. Additionally, maintain a digital or physical duplicate of your insurance data with you during your trips.

Planning your trip to the Isles of Scilly in 2023-2024 takes careful consideration of the ideal time to travel, transportation alternatives, admission requirements, and packing needs. By planning sufficiently and remaining informed, you can make the most of your island vacation and guarantee a smooth and pleasurable travel.

III. ACCOMMODATION

When visiting the Isles of Scilly, selecting the correct lodging may substantially improve your experience. The islands provide a broad choice of housing alternatives, appealing to various interests and budgets. Here, we examine the many kinds of lodgings accessible for your visit.

A. Hotels and Resorts

For guests seeking comfort and convenience, hotels and resorts in the Isles of Scilly give a good option. These places provide a variety of facilities and services, providing a comfortable and delightful visit.

- **St. Mary's Hall Hotel:** Located on St. Mary's Island, this lovely hotel provides spectacular sea views and comfortable accommodations. Guests may relax in the lounge, taste locally produced food, and take advantage of the hotel's closeness to Hugh Town.

- **Karma St. Martin's:** Situated on the scenic St. Martin's Island, this luxury resort gives a calm vacation. With spa facilities, exquisite cuisine, and easy access to stunning beaches, it's ideal for a romantic weekend or a revitalizing retreat.

B. Bed and Breakfasts

Bed and breakfasts (B&Bs) are a popular alternative for individuals searching for a pleasant and inviting ambience. They give a personal touch and the chance to engage with local hosts.

- **Carnwethers Country House:** This beautiful B&B on St. Mary's Island provides comfortable accommodations and a full breakfast to start your day. It's surrounded by gorgeous gardens and is within walking distance of the port and town.

- **Tregarthen's Hotel B&B**: Located on the waterfront in St. Mary's, Tregarthen's provides not only pleasant accommodations but also spectacular sea views. Guests may enjoy a full breakfast and convenient access to the island's attractions.

C. Self-Catering Cottages

If you want a more autonomous experience or are traveling with a group or family, self-catering cottages are an ideal alternative. They give a home away from home, complete with cooking amenities.

- **Scilly Cottages**: Scilly Cottages provides a broad range of self-catering accommodations around the islands, from historic cottages to contemporary flats. This option enables you to make your schedule and dine at your leisure.

- **Island Cottage Holidays**: Another wonderful alternative for self-catering choices, Island Cottage Holidays has a selection of cottages that suit various party sizes and tastes. Many houses come with amazing sea views.

D. Camping and Glamping Options

For those wanting a more rustic and immersing experience in nature, camping and glamping (glamorous camping) alternatives are available on the Isles of Scilly.

- **Troytown Campsite:** Located on the secluded St. Agnes Island, Troytown Campsite provides classic camping and glamping accommodations. Campers may wake up to stunning sea views and have easy access to the island's natural beauties.

- **Karma St. Martin's Glamping:** If you're searching for a deluxe camping experience, Karma St. Martin's provides glamping choices, including safari tents with contemporary facilities. It's a unique way to interact with nature without compromising comfort.

No matter the sort of accommodation you pick, reserving in advance, particularly during the busy season, is suggested to ensure your stay. Each choice provides a different experience, enabling you to adapt your vacation to the Isles of Scilly to your interests, whether it's a calm seaside resort, a comfortable bed and breakfast, a self-catering cottage, or an adventurous camping trip among breathtaking surroundings.

IV. GETTING AROUND

When touring the Isles of Scilly, traversing the islands is a vital part of the experience. Here, we look into the numerous transportation choices available to make the most of your island-hopping experience.

A. Transportation on the Isles

The Isles of Scilly are fortunate with a tiny and personal transportation network that contributes to the attractiveness of these islands. While the major means of travel is walking, there are a few more choices to assist you in getting around:

- **Island Hopping:** With each island being relatively near to the others, you may tour various islands throughout your vacation. Ferries and boat services operate often, making it simple to get from one island to another.

- **Taxis**: There are taxis accessible on the islands, particularly on St. Mary's. They are a simple method to reach your hotel or explore the island's attractions.

- **Buses**: St. Mary's offers a limited bus service that may transport you to different regions of the island. This is a cost-effective approach to reach various regions.

B. Rental Cars and Bicycles

One distinctive element of the Isles of Scilly is the lack of private automobiles. There are no automobile rentals available on the islands.

However, you may hire golf buggies, which are electric vehicles suitable for island touring.

Bicycles are another popular choice for moving about. They let you explore the islands at your speed, enjoying the stunning vistas and uncovering hidden jewels. Bicycles are widely available for hire, and many lodgings supply them as part of your stay.

C. Boat Tours and Water Taxis

One of the most thrilling ways to visit the Isles of Scilly is by taking advantage of boat trips and water taxis. These choices allow access to secluded beaches, animal observation possibilities, and unique island experiences:

- **Boat trips:** Various businesses provide boat trips that take you to some of the most beautiful and secluded areas in the archipelago. From nature cruises where you may view seals and seabirds to history tours investigating shipwrecks and old villages, there's a boat tour for every interest.

- **Water Taxis**: Water taxis are a simple method to transit between islands fast. They are also available for bespoke journeys, ensuring you can reach your selected locations comfortably and efficiently.

One highly recommended activity is taking a glass-bottom boat excursion. These trips give a fascinating viewpoint on the underwater environment of the Isles of Scilly, enabling you to observe marine life and dynamic bottom ecosystems without getting wet.

In conclusion, the Isles of Scilly provide a unique and beautiful transit network that enriches the whole experience of island exploring. Whether you want to island-hop, hire a golf buggy or bicycle, or go on boat excursions and water taxis, you'll have the chance to experience the natural beauty and quiet of these magnificent islands from numerous vantage points.

V. TOP ATTRACTIONS

The Isles of Scilly are a treasure trove of natural beauty, history, and cultural legacy. In this part, we'll examine some of the main attractions that make these islands a distinct and engaging visit.

1. St. Mary's Island

St. Mary's, the biggest of the Isles of Scilly, serves as the major entrance for travelers and provides a multitude of attractions:

- **Hugh Town:** The island's capital, Hugh Town, is a delightful center including stores, cafés, restaurants, and galleries. It's a wonderful site to start your investigation of St. Mary's.

- **The Garrison**: This historic landmark, originally erected to fight against Spanish invasion in the 16th century, provides panoramic views of the neighboring islands and is home to the Star Castle, a well-preserved stronghold turned hotel.

- **Porthcressa Beach:** A magnificent crescent-shaped beach suitable for sunbathing and swimming.

- **Tresco and Bryher:** These islands are readily accessible from St. Mary's by boat, and they provide their distinct charms, which we'll explore later.

2. Tresco Abbey Garden

Tresco, the second-largest island, is famed for the Tresco Abbey Garden, a floral wonderland that attracts people from across the globe. Highlights include:

- **Exotic Plants:** Explore this subtropical garden boasting a wonderful collection of exotic plants and flowers from across the world. The garden's microclimate enables species to grow that wouldn't survive elsewhere in the UK.

- **Valhalla Museum**: Located on the grounds, this museum contains an unusual collection of shipwrecked figureheads and other marine antiquities.

- **Walking Trails**: Wander around the nicely groomed walkways and enjoy calm moments surrounded by bright vegetation.

3. St. Martin's Vineyard

St. Martin's Island, frequently referred to as the "Teardrop of Scilly," is noted for its gorgeous beaches and the St. Martin's Vineyard. Here's what to expect:

- **Vineyard Tours**: Explore the vineyard and winery, where you may taste locally made wines and learn about the winemaking process.

- **Crystal Clear sea**: St. Martin's has some of the purest seas in the UK, making it a perfect site for snorkeling, paddleboarding, or just lounging on the beach.

- **Quaint town**: Visit the lovely town with its white houses, friendly residents, and a feeling of timelessness.

4. Beaches and Coastal Walks

The Isles of Scilly are a delight for beach lovers and hikers. Some of the most magnificent beaches and coastline hikes include:

- **Great Bay (St. Martin's):** This broad bay provides white dunes and turquoise seas, great for swimming and sunbathing.

- **Pentle Bay (Tresco):** Known for its vast sandy shoreline and views of Shipman Head and Round Island Lighthouse.

- **The South West Coast Path:** This route provides beautiful panoramas and the chance to observe animals, including seals and seagulls.

5. Historical Sites

The Isles of Scilly possess a rich history, with several well-preserved historical places to explore:

- **Cromwell's Castle (Tresco):** Built during the English Civil War, this coastal artillery fort gives outstanding views of the surrounding islands.

- **King Charles's Castle (Tresco):** Another old structure, this castle is set on a hill and affords panoramic views of the archipelago.

- **Old Town:** Explore the old village on St. Mary's, boasting medieval houses, a church going back to the 12th century, and the interesting Harry's Walls, a defensive construction.

These top attractions are only a peek of the treasures awaiting you in the Isles of Scilly. Whether you're attracted to the natural beauty, historical landmarks, or cultural events, the Isles provide a thrilling trip through time and nature.

VI. ACTIVITIES AND ADVENTURES

The Isles of Scilly, with their pure seas and magnificent scenery, offer a broad selection of activities and excursions for nature aficionados and outdoor explorers alike. Here's a peak into some of the intriguing alternatives available:

1. Scuba Diving and Snorkeling

The crystal-clear seas around the Isles of Scilly create an underwater paradise for scuba divers and snorkelers. Here's what you may expect:

- **Maritime Life:** Explore vivid maritime environments filled with colorful fish, lively seals, and unique coral species. The Isles are recognised for their great visibility, making them a wonderful place for underwater photography.

- **Wrecks and Reefs:** Discover shipwrecks and underwater reefs, some going back centuries. The islands' seafaring history provides an added dimension of excitement to these diving adventures.

- **Diving facilities**: Professional diving facilities on St. Mary's and surrounding islands provide equipment rental, guided dives, and instruction for divers of all abilities.

2. Bird Watching

The Isles of Scilly are a paradise for birdwatchers, drawing ornithologists and enthusiasts from throughout the globe. Key features include:

- **Migratory Birds:** The islands serve as a significant stopover for migratory birds, particularly during spring and fall. Witness the sight of thousands of birds going by.

- **Breeding Colonies:** Observe seabird colonies on the cliffs and offshore islands, including puffins, gannets, and kittiwakes.

- **Guided excursions**: Local guides provide birding excursions, offering insights into the varied avian species and their habitats.

3. Kayaking and Paddleboarding

Exploring the Isles of Scilly from the boat is a tranquil and engaging experience. Kayaking and paddleboarding possibilities abound:

- **Coastal Routes**: Paddle around the craggy coastline, seeking secret coves, sea caves, and isolated beaches. Keep a lookout for seals and other aquatic animals.

- **Guided trips**: Join guided kayaking or paddle boarding trips for a safe and educational journey. Knowledgeable guides will discuss local tales and point out natural beauties.

- **Equipment Rental:** Rent kayaks or paddle boards from outfitters on several islands, and go on your self-guided water tour.

4. Fishing Excursions

Fishing aficionados will find an insufficient opportunity to cast their hooks and pull in some of the freshest catches:

- **Deep-Sea Fishing:** Join deep-sea fishing expeditions to capture a variety of fish species, including mackerel, pollack, and bass. Experienced guides supply equipment and recommendations.

- **Fly Fishing:** Explore freshwater streams and ponds for trout and other freshwater species. Fly fishing is a relaxing way to connect with nature.

- **Cook Your Catch:** Many lodgings and local eateries provide the opportunity to cook your freshly caught fish, creating a delightful and genuine island dining experience.

5. Cycling Routes

Exploring the Isles of Scilly on two wheels gives a leisurely approach to take in the stunning landscapes:

- **Bike Rentals:** Rent bicycles around the islands, including electric bikes for an easier ride on steep terrain.

- **Gorgeous Routes:** Pedal along gorgeous coastal pathways, discover natural reserves, and visit historical monuments while enjoying the fresh sea air.

- **Island-Hopping by Bike:** Combine cycling with island-hopping by bringing your bike on inter-island ferries, enabling you to tour various islands in a single day.

Whether you're seeking undersea experiences, birding, serene water sports, fishing expeditions, or leisurely cycling through gorgeous landscapes, the Isles of Scilly provides a variety of activities and excursions to make your stay unforgettable. Each encounter delivers a fresh perspective on the islands' natural beauty and cultural legacy.

VII. DINING AND CUISINE

Exploring the gastronomic marvels of the Isles of Scilly is a great excursion in itself. The islands provide a unique combination of fresh local products, seafood, and a splash of foreign influence, ensuring that every meal is a remarkable experience.

A. Local Food Specialties

The Isles of Scilly are recognised for their scrumptious native delicacies that encapsulate the spirit of island life:

- **Scillonian Crab**: Crab fishing is an important business here, and you'll find crab on the menu in numerous forms, from crab sandwiches to crab salads. It's a must-try delicacy.

- **New Potatoes:** Grown in the sandy soil of the islands, new potatoes are soft and tasty. They're commonly served as a side dish, including seafood.

- **Duchy Gin**: Produced on St. Mary's, this native gin incorporates botanicals unique to the Isles, including gorse flowers and sea salt. It's the ideal companion to a pleasant drink.

B. Restaurants and Pubs

Discovering local cuisines is a delight on the Isles of Scilly, owing to the diversity of attractive eateries and hospitable pubs:

- **The Beach**: This renowned restaurant on Porthmellon Beach, St. Mary's, provides a broad cuisine with a focus on

48

seafood. Enjoy your dinner while staring out at the gorgeous coastal vistas.

- **The Turks Head:** Located in the center of St. Agnes, this historic pub provides typical pub meals and boasts a pleasant environment, making it a favorite with residents and tourists alike.

- **The Ruin Beach café:** Situated on Tresco, this beachside café provides a Mediterranean-inspired meal with an abundance of fresh, locally produced foods. It's a lovely place for a leisurely supper.

C. Dining with a View

One of the most wonderful parts of eating on the Isles of Scilly is the ability to taste your meal amid stunning vistas:

- **Juliet's Garden Restaurant**: Nestled on a rocky outcrop of St. Mary's, this restaurant has magnificent sea views. Enjoy a romantic meal or a relaxing lunch on the balcony while watching the boats pass by.

- **Fraggle Rock pub**: Perched on a hill on Bryher, this pub provides amazing views of Tresco and the neighboring islands. It's the best place for sundowners and viewing the sunset.

- **Karma St. Martin's:** The resort's restaurant on St. Martin's Island not only serves wonderful food but also enjoys spectacular sea views. Savor your dinner while watching the peaceful waters of Teän Sound.

Dining on the Isles of Scilly is a delight for the senses, with each meal delivering a combination of native tastes, fresh ingredients, and stunning vistas. Whether you're having a crab feast, drinking locally created gin, or savoring a lunch with a seaside background, your culinary experiences here will be nothing short of extraordinary.

VIII. SHOPPING

Exploring the dynamic retail environment on the Isles of Scilly is a chance to find unusual souvenirs, local crafts, fresh vegetables, and breathtaking art pieces. Here's what you can look forward to:

A. Souvenirs and Local Crafts

Bringing home a piece of the Isles of Scilly is a valued feature of each visit. The islands provide a broad choice of souvenirs and locally produced items:

- **Seashell Jewelry**: Craftsmen on the Isles produce magnificent jewelry from shells, pearls, and other treasures from the surrounding seas. These items make for lovely souvenirs.

- **Scilly fragrances:** Fragrance manufacturers on the islands create perfumes, soaps, and candles inspired by the fragrances of the sea and native flora. They encapsulate the spirit of the Isles in a bottle.

- **Handmade Pottery:** Skilled potters manufacture unique ceramic pieces with island themes, marine life, and coastal sceneries. Functional and beautiful, these objects make wonderfully memorable presents.

B. Farmers' Markets

Visiting the various farmers' markets in the Isles of Scilly is a lovely opportunity to immerse yourself in island life and sample fresh, locally produced produce:

- **St. Mary's Farmers' Market**: Held weekly on St. Mary's Island, this market offers a diversity of island-grown fruits, vegetables, herbs, and artisanal items. Don't miss the chance to enjoy locally created cheeses, jams, and chutneys.

- **St. Agnes Community Market**: On St. Agnes Island, this community market provides a range of fresh food, handcrafted items, and crafts. It's a terrific location to meet local farmers and craftspeople.

C. Art Galleries

The natural beauty of the Isles of Scilly has long inspired artists, and you may explore their works at the local art galleries:

- **Phoenix Craft Workshops and Gallery:** Located on St. Mary's, this gallery shows an excellent selection of local art, including paintings, jewelry ray, and sculptures. It's a fantastic spot to discover a unique piece of art that reminds you of your stay.

- **Bryher Gallery**: Situated on Bryher Island, this gallery displays the work of local artists who take inspiration from the spectacular landscapes and seascapes of the Isles. The ever-changing exhibitions guarantee there's always something fresh to explore.

- **Wildlife painting gallery:** Located on Tresco, this gallery specializes in wildlife and natural history paintings. You'll discover a broad assortment of artwork showcasing the great biodiversity of the Isles.

Exploring the shopping options on the Isles of Scilly is not only about obtaining souvenirs; it's an opportunity to interact with the local culture, support artists and farmers, and carry a piece of these wonderful islands back home with you. Whether you're seeking a handcrafted trinket, fresh island vegetables, or a piece of art that depicts the beauty of the Isles, the shopping experiences here are as distinctive and unforgettable as the location itself.

IX. EVENTS AND FESTIVALS

The Isles of Scilly come alive with a dynamic schedule of events and festivals that highlight the islands' distinctive culture, environment, and creative legacy. Here are some of the noteworthy events you can look forward to:

1. Isles of Scilly Walking Festival

The Isles of Scilly Walking Festival is a monument to the islands' outstanding natural surroundings and gives a terrific chance to explore on foot. This yearly event, generally held in April, brings together walkers and environment lovers from across the globe. Highlights include:

- **Guided excursions:** Expert guides accompany participants on a range of guided excursions, from coastal hikes to historical studies.

- **Animals Encounters:** As spring approaches, the islands come alive with animals. The event frequently features wildlife-focused treks, where you may view seagulls, seals, and other natural animals.

- **Cultural Insights**: Learn about the islands' history, archaeology, and folklore from qualified guides who share their enthusiasm for the Isles of Scilly.

2. Tresco Island Abbey Garden Events

Tresco Abbey Garden, a botanical masterpiece on Tresco Island, organizes events throughout the year that celebrate nature, horticulture, and the arts. Some important occurrences include:

- **Garden Walks:** Join guided walks of the Abbey Garden, where you may examine the wide array of plants and learn about their cultivation in this unique setting.

- **Open Air Theatre:** Experience the wonder of live performances set against the background of the garden's magnificent scenery. The garden typically holds outdoor theatrical plays throughout the summer months.

- **Art exhibits:** Tresco's link to the arts is recognised via art exhibits and events that display the work of local and visiting artists.

3. Art Scilly Week

Art Scilly Week is a bright celebration of the creative talent that lives in the Isles of Scilly. Held yearly in May, this festival brings artists, craftspeople, and art aficionados together. Highlights include:

- **Art Trails**: Explore open studios and galleries around the islands, affording an insight into the eclectic art culture of Scilly.

- **Workshops**: Participate in hands-on workshops and learn from local artists who specialize in different media, from painting to ceramics.

- **Exhibitions**: Discover the innovative works of both young and experienced artists, frequently inspired by the stunning scenery of the Isles.

These events and festivals give you a chance to immerse yourself in the distinctive culture and natural beauty of the Isles of Scilly. Whether you're interested in trekking through pristine landscapes, seeing botanical marvels, or basking in creative inspiration, the islands have plenty to offer year-round. Be sure to check the event calendars and schedule your vacation to coincide with these interesting activities.

X. PRACTICAL INFORMATION

When arranging your journey to the Isles of Scilly, it's crucial to have practical information at your fingertips to guarantee a smooth and pleasurable experience. Here's a detailed resource to assist you with money and banking, health and safety recommendations, communication and internet access, and emergency contacts:

A. Currency and Banking

- **Currency**: The official currency of the Isles of Scilly, like the rest of the United Kingdom, is the British Pound Sterling (£). While some shops may take major credit and debit cards, it's good to carry extra cash, particularly for little transactions and in case you visit establishments that do not accept cards.

- **ATMs**: You may locate ATMs (cash machines) on St. Mary's Island, the major center of the Isles. It's a good idea to withdraw cash before you go to Sto Mary's to guarantee you have enough for your stay on the smaller islands.

- **Banks**: There are no main street banks on the smaller islands. If you desire banking services beyond simple cash withdrawals, you will need to visit a bank on the mainland before your trip.

B. Health and Safety Tips

- **Healthcare**: The Isles of Scilly features a well-equipped health facility on St. Mary's Island, offering medical services. However, it's wise to bring any vital prescriptions with you, since certain prescription drugs may not be easily accessible.

- **Emergency Services**: Dial 999 for emergencies. The islands offer a good ambulance service and hospital facilities.

- **Sun Protection:** When visiting during the summer, apply sunscreen, wear a hat, and remain hydrated, since the sun may be powerful despite the moderate environment.

- **Sea Safety**: If you want to participate in water activities, be cautious of tides and currents. Always observe safety requirements, wear adequate clothing, and consider guided tours for specific activities.

C. Communication and Internet Access

- **Mobile Phone Coverage**: Mobile phone coverage is typically strong on St. Mary's Island. However, signal strength may vary on the smaller, more secluded islands.

- **Internet connectivity:** Most lodgings, restaurants, and cafés on the major islands have Wi-Fi connectivity. However, owing to the islands' isolated position, the internet connection may not be as fast or dependable as what you're used to on the mainland.

D. Emergency Contacts

- **Emergency Services:** In case of a life-threatening emergency or urgent medical help, phone 999. This number links you to the police, fire, ambulance, and other emergency services.

- **Coastguard**: If you're at sea and want help, call the Coastguard on VHF Channel 16 or ring 999 and ask for the Coastguard.

- **St. Mary's Hospital:** The major hospital in the Isles of Scilly may be contacted at +44 (0)1720 422392.

- **Non-Emergency Police:** For non-emergency police problems, call the local police station on St. Mary's at +44 (0)1720 422444.

- **Pharmacy**: There is a pharmacy on St. Mary's Island, which may be contacted at +44 (0)1720 422439.

- **Tourist Information Center**: The Isles of Scilly Tourist Information Center can give support and information throughout your stay. They may be contacted at +44 (0)1720 620600.

Visiting the Isles of Scilly is a unique and magical experience, but being prepared with practical knowledge is crucial to making the most of your vacation. Whether it's understanding the local currency, being safe, staying connected, or knowing who to contact in case of an emergency, these practical suggestions can help guarantee an enjoyable and worry-free vacation to this distant and magnificent region.

XI. ITINERARIES (2023)

Planning your plan for a vacation to the Isles of Scilly in 2023 you were immersing yourself in the natural beauty, culture, and activities the islands have to offer. Here's a recommended agenda for a wonderful visit:

Day 1: Arrival at St. Mary's

- **Morning**: Arrive at St. Mary's Airport, either by aircraft from the mainland or by passenger ferry from Penzance. Take in the gorgeous scenery as you approach the islands.

- **Afternoon**: Check in to your lodgings on St. Mary's, the biggest and major island. Spend the day touring Hugh Town, the island's quaint capital. Stroll around the waterfront and have lunch at one of the local eateries.

- **Evening**: Relax and relax in your hotel, savoring your first night on the Isles of Scilly.

Day 2-3: Exploring St. Mary's

- **Full Days**: Dedicate these two days to touring St. Mary's. Visit historical sights like the Garrison and Old Town, visit the gorgeous beaches such as Porthcressa, and enjoy a stroll along the coastal trails.

- **Lunch**: Try fresh fish at one of the local eateries or opt for a typical Cornish pasty from a local bakery.

- **Afternoons**: Visit the Isles of Scilly Museum to learn about the islands' history and culture. If you're a nature enthusiast, don't miss the opportunity to view seabirds and seals along the shore.

- **Evenings**: Dine at a beachside restaurant and enjoy the island's quiet ambience.

Day 4: Tresco Island Adventure

- **Morning**: Take a boat from St. Mary's to Tresco Island. Spend the morning touring the world-renowned Tresco Abbey Garden, containing exotic flora and breathtaking scenery.

- **Lunch:** Enjoy lunch at the Ruin Beach Cafe, overlooking the sea.

- **Afternoon**: Discover more of Tesco's natural splendor by visiting its beaches, especially Pentle Bay, and possibly hire a bicycle for island exploration.

- **Evening**: Return to St. Mary's for a delicious meal at a local restaurant.

Day 5: St. Martin's Excursion

- **Morning**: Embark on a boat excursion to St. Martin's Island. Begin your day with a visit to the St. Martin's Vineyard, where you can learn about winemaking and drink locally locally-made

- **Lunch**: Enjoy a picnic on one of the island's gorgeous beaches.

- **Afternoon**: Take a stroll through the island's picturesque pathways, admiring its unspoilt beauty.

- **Evening**: Return to St. Mary's and dine at one of the island's charming cafés.

Day 6-7: Exploring Other Islands

- **Full Days**: Dedicate the remaining two days to island-hopping excursions. Take boats to visit the lesser islands including St. Agnes, Bryher, and more. Each island has its distinct beauty, scenery, and activities.

- **Activities**: Engage in varied activities, from birding on St. Agnes to investigating the shipwrecks on Bryher.

- **Lunch**: Savor picnics or eat at local cafés and bars on the smaller islands.

- **Evenings**: Return to St. Mary's to unwind, taste local food, and reflect on your island-hopping excursions.

This schedule delivers a well-rounded experience of the Isles of Scilly, from touring the main island to traveling to the smaller ones. Be careful to check for any particular event dates or seasonal considerations when arranging your visit to make the most of your vacation to these magnificent and distinctive islands.

XII. ITINERARY UPDATE (2024)

For anyone considering a repeat visit to the Isles of Scilly in 2024 or searching for a revised itinerary, there are exciting developments, new attractions, and special events to consider. Here's an updated itinerary with the newest facts and recommendations:

Day 1: Arrival at St. Mary's

- **Morning**: Arrive at St. Mary's Airport, or take the passenger ferry from Penzance. Witness the ageless splendor of the islands as you approach.

- **Afternoon**: Check in to your lodgings on St. Mary's. Begin your journey with a visit to the newly opened Isles of Scilly Welcome Center, where you can acquire the latest information on island activities and attractions.

- **Evening**: Enjoy supper at one of the island's famed seafood restaurants, such as Juliet's Garden Restaurant, for a pleasant start to your vacation.

Day 2-3: Exploring St. Mary's

- **Full Days**: Dedicate the first two days to rediscovering St. Mary's, but this time, explore the newly added attractions like the St. Mary's Botanic Garden, a calm haven of native and exotic species.

- **Lunch**: Sample local food at freshly launched cafes like "The Greenhouse," famed for its farm-to-table eating experience.

- **Afternoons**: Visit the revamped Isles of Scilly Museum, which now provides interactive displays and a more immersive look at the islands' background.

- **Evenings**: Try the newest blend of island cuisines at inventive eateries that have popped up, combining traditional dishes with global influences.

Day 4: Tresco Island Adventure

- **Morning**: Take a ferry to Tresco Island and see Tresco Abbey Garden to observe any new additions or alterations in the garden's design.
- **Lunch**: Savor lunch at the recently opened "Tresco Beach Club," a

sophisticated beachside restaurant with breathtaking sea views.

- **Afternoon**: Explore the extended network of riding paths on Tresco, with bike rental facilities now providing electric bikes for an easier ride.

- **Evening**: Dine at "The Ruin Beach Cafe" for a sample of the newest culinary innovations inspired by the island's natural richness.

Day 5: St. Martin's Excursion

- **Morning**: Hop on a boat to St. Martin's Island and enjoy the newly inaugurated "St. Martin's Vineyard Experience," where you may assist in grape picking and winemaking.

- **Lunch**: Relish a gourmet picnic box with locally produced products from "Island Delights," a new cuisine business on St. Martin's.

- **Afternoon**: Explore the newest walking routes and views that have been opened up on the island, affording even more stunning perspectives.

- **Evening**: Return to St. Mary's and eat at a modern restaurant, recognised for its combination of foreign and island cuisines.

Day 6-7: Exploring Other Islands

- **Full Days**: Spend the last two days touring the smaller islands, including the new nature reserve on St. Agnes, home to rare flora and animals.

- **Activities**: Participate in freshly offered activities like guided kayaking trips to sea caves on Bryher or join a glass-bottom boat tour to observe colorful underwater life.

- **Lunch**: Enjoy exquisite lunches created by local craftsmen, showcasing the freshest island products.

- **Evenings**: Return to St. Mary's and unwind at one of the freshly remodeled lodgings, featuring contemporary conveniences and island charm.

As you explore the Isles of Scilly in 2024, you'll discover an expanded experience with new attractions, eating choices, and activities that reflect the islands' dedication to maintaining their natural beauty while embracing innovation and modern culture. Be sure to check for any unique events in 2024, such as art festivals or wildlife conservation efforts, to enrich your itinerary further.

XIII. CONCLUSION

In finishing your voyage through the Isles of Scilly, you've embarked on a fascinating adventure packed with stunning vistas, unique cultural experiences, and a profound connection to nature. The Isles of Scilly provide a quiet getaway from the rush and bustle of daily life, affording a look into a world where time appears to stand still.

Throughout your trip, you've explored the clean beaches, traveled along gorgeous coastal roads, and marveled at the floral delights of Tresco Abbey Garden. You've tasted the delights of fresh seafood, had picnics on isolated beaches, and learned the rich history and culture of the islands.

As you wave goodbye to this magical archipelago, your memories of the Isles of Scilly will stay inscribed in your heart. You could find yourself thinking about future travel plans, possibly returning to discover new sights, attend special events, or just reconnect with the tranquil beauty of these islands.

Whether you're heading out on your next trip or cherishing the memories of your time on the Isles of Scilly, the captivating charm of these islands will continue to call, beckoning you to return and create new experiences in this lovely corner of the globe. Until then, may your journeys be filled with wonder, discovery, and the timeless charm of the Isles of Scilly. Safe travels, and may your future adventures be as rewarding as this one.

Printed in Great Britain
by Amazon